is for Hu
A Modern Parent's ABC

Joel Rickett & Spencer Wilson

PENGUIN BOOKS

For Sophie, Esme, Gracie and Isla,
who finish all their hummus – sometimes.

Au pair

Aa

Aromatherapy

Aa

App

Bb

Balance bike

Baby carrier

Babyccino

Cc

Carrot sticks

Calpol

Catchment

Controlled crying

Dd

Dough balls

Drama

Equipped (for everything)

Electric toothbrush

Ee

Expecting

Eco-friendly

4x4

Face paint

Ff

Gg

Grobag

Growth spurt

Hummus

Hugh
(Fearnley-Whittingstall)

Hunter wellies

Hh

Helicopter
parenting

Ii

iPaddy

Jj

Jute bag

Ju-jitsu

Kinaesthetic learning

Ketchup

TOM TOM

Kk

Low-cost airline

Latching on

Ll

Loft conversion

Mm

Muslin

Monitor

Nn

Naughty step

Nature
deficit
disorder

No!

Night feed

Ofsted
(outstanding)

Oo

Ocado

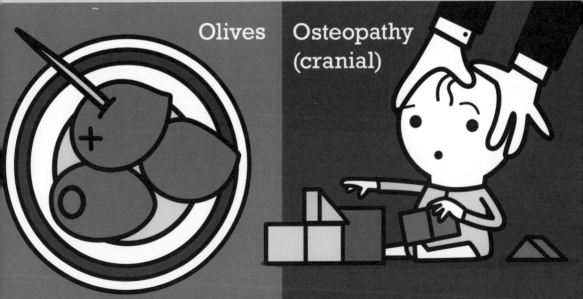

Olives

Osteopathy
(cranial)

Pp

Playdate

Purée

Q q

Quinoa

Regifting

TO: ~~Jack~~ Harry

Reward chart

Rr

Rhymetime

Rice cakes

Ss

Squeezed middle

Scooter (micro)

Swaddle

Soft play

Tt

Trunki

TENS machine

Time out

Tummy time

Unreasonable

Vaccination

Uu

Ultrasound

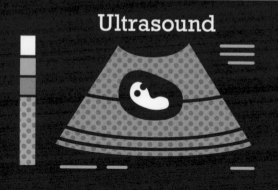

Vv

Vitamins

Violin lessons

Ww

Wheat intolerant

Xmas excess

Xx

Yy

Yoghurt
(probiotic)

Yummy mummy

Zumba

Zzzz

Zz

Joel Rickett

is a publisher and a (very) occasional writer.
His previous books include *How to Avoid Huge Ships* and *Whitstable Mum in Custard Shortage*. He lives in north London (of course), where he's a thoroughly modern parent to two gorgeous, demanding girls.

GONE TO UNCH

ModernABC.co.uk

Spencer Wilson

is an illustrator and co-founder of the illustration, design and
animation company Peepshow Collective. He has been working to commission
since 1998 in a world of coffee cups and ordered chaos; his work follows this theme
with the creation of sketchy ideas and twisted thoughts. He lives in the modern
parenting paradise that is Berkhamsted, Hertfordshire, with his wife
and two girls, who never cease to inspire him.

www.spencerwilson.co.uk   www.peepshow.org.uk

PENGUIN BOOKS

Published by the Penguin Group

Penguin Books Ltd, 80 Strand, London WC2R 0RL, England

Penguin Group (USA) Inc., 375 Hudson Street, New York, New York 10014, USA

Penguin Group (Canada), 90 Eglinton Avenue East, Suite 700, Toronto, Ontario, Canada M4P 2Y3
(a division of Pearson Penguin Canada Inc.)

Penguin Ireland, 25 St Stephen's Green, Dublin 2, Ireland
(a division of Penguin Books Ltd)

Penguin Group (Australia), 707 Collins Street, Melbourne, Victoria 3008, Australia
(a division of Pearson Australia Group Pty Ltd)

Penguin Books India Pvt Ltd, 11 Community Centre,
Panchsheel Park, New Delhi – 110 017, India

Penguin Group (NZ), 67 Apollo Drive, Rosedale, Auckland 0632, New Zealand
(a division of Pearson New Zealand Ltd)

Penguin Books (South Africa) (Pty) Ltd, Block D, Rosebank Office Park,
181 Jan Smuts Avenue, Parktown North, Gauteng 2193, South Africa

Penguin Books Ltd, Registered Offices: 80 Strand, London WC2R 0RL, England

www.penguin.com

First published by Viking 2013
Published in Penguin Books 2014
001

Set in Rockwell, Sasson and Frutiger
Designed by Spencer Wilson
Printed in China

ISBN: 978–0–241–97123–9